What is Your Life?

By

Dr. Randy Hilton

This book considers what your life is according to the Scripture. The Scripture compares our lives to things that we can easily understand. While this is not a thorough treatise to the study, the author does believe that it will provide some insight and food for thought. Consider, What is your Life?

This

is your life

A Tale that is Told

James 4:14 asks the question, "What is your life?"
In Psalms 90:9 we are told that our life is a tale that is told.
"For all your days are passed away in thy wrath; we spend
our years as a tale that is told."

Our life is a story. This story can be traced back
through generations: our genealogy. We can learn about
how our parents met and their story of life. We can even go

back to when their parents met, and so on. We often look at pictures of when we were very young and ask questions. We get our parents and siblings to help fill in the gaps of what our memory lacks. Our story will develop and add chapters as we live our lives. But even like a great book, it has an ending. At least our life has an ending as far as this world is concerned. We know that the story continues into eternity. But as far as this life, the story, even if it is a long one filled with several chapters, it does come to an end. And, when we get to the end of the story, it will seem like it did not take us very long to get there. How often we think to ourselves, "that seems like just yesterday", when, in fact, it could have been several years ago.

When you think about your life, your tale, your story, what kind of story is it? What is your story? Fact or fiction. Real or façade. What is it really or do we try to make it what we want everyone to think it is? It is important to be honest about what your life really is.

What will people remember? Lord, help me. What will they say when they find out I have passed away? When my name brings back memories to their mind, what will those memories be? What will stick out in their minds? What will be the first thing that comes to their minds? What do I want them to remember? How do I want to be remembered? What will I do to make that memory be what I want it to be?

Why do we celebrate Memorial Day? We celebrate Memorial Day so that we can remember the lives of those who have gone on before us. Primarily, we remember those who gave their lives in service of their country. Those who died to protect and defend their country are remembered. We do not want them to be forgotten. One of the main reasons is because we do not want to be forgotten ourselves. When we pass in death, will there be anyone who will remember us? Will there be anyone who sets around and reminisces about my life? Our lives are very short, so, in a way, we want our lives or at least the story of them, to be retold and not forgotten. When your family and friends remember you, what about you will they remember the most?

We all have a tale that we tell. It is called our life. From the moment we are born until our last breath we are living out our life, telling our tale. It is the hyphen between the birth and death dates that tell what and how we lived. What does/will your hyphen say?

My life is like a tale that's been told

A journey of laughter, joy and woe

Experiences that make me bold

And a path that I still do not know

Memories of a life well-lived

Of trials and triumphs I have seen

The joys of life that I have sieved

The lessons I've learned in between

A story of sorrow and of glee

Of times that have gone

And of love that will be

Of courage and strength

To keep me on my feet

My life is like a tale that's been told indeed - Anonymous

A Pilgrimage

James 4:14 asks, "What is your life?" Psalms 119:54 answers, "Thy statutes have been my songs in the house of my pilgrimage." Psalms 39:12 states, "Hear my prayer, O Lord, and give ear unto my cry; hold not thy peace at my tears: for I am a stranger with thee, and a sojourner, as all my fathers were."

Our life is a pilgrimage in which we are headed towards eternity. Everyone of us will spend eternity somewhere. From the moment we were conceived, we began our pilgrimage towards it. Since there are two possible destinations, which one will it be? I know that I will spend eternity with Christ since I have put my faith and trust in Him alone. I hope that you can say the same.

This life is a personal pilgrimage. This is personal. This is my life. Everything about it is personal. My family, my friends, my choices, my successes, my failures, my mistakes, all are personal. I am making my way through all these personal issues, relationships, and events, making my way home. No one should say this is not personal. It cannot be anything else but personal.

Part of my pilgrimage has been my marriage. I have been with my wife more than half of my life. I have been with her more than I have not been with her. This relationship has been a huge part of my pilgrimage. Our lives together have produced three children. We have a young lady who feels very much like our own child. She and her husband have three children. They have been a part of my pilgrimage for more than twenty years now.

This pilgrimage is an eternal one. That is, even when this life is over, eternity really then begins. As I travel this life, I must think of the extending of life into eternity. I cannot just think about right now. I must think of eternity. This is true for me, but also for others. When I look at another person: student, child, spouse, sibling, I must see them as an eternal being. This person is going to live somewhere for eternity.

In my pilgrimage I will do a lot of things. Some of these things will be very personal and center around me. Other things I do will be spiritual and center around my spiritual person and my relationship with the Holy Spirit. I will spend a lot of time working. I will have a lot of co-workers who are eternal beings. Do I care where they will spend eternity?

I am married. I care very deeply about my wife. My main concern for her is that she will truly follow after Christ. I know that she is a Christian. I know where she will spend eternity. It makes this pilgrimage so much easier having her by my side and we both being on the same page spiritually and eternally.

My pilgrimage has included the Lord blessing my wife and I with three children. They have been a blessing to us as we have had the privilege of seeing them come to the Lord, be trained and equipped in their education, and now, watching as the Lord reveals His will to them and they follow after Him. They will continue to be a part of my pilgrimage until the Lord calls me home. I look forward to grandchildren if the Lord allows and seeing them come to the Lord as well. I imagine all of us in heaven together one day.

As I think about my pilgrimage, I think of the questions: are we making any progress? Are we getting anywhere? Where are we headed? How do we know where to go? How is it that we will get there? All of these questions and I am sure many more will need to be asked and answered as we assess our pilgrimage and determine where to go next.

Just like for any journey, we must get ready for this pilgrimage. How do I get ready for a journey? I need to make sure that I have everything I need for the trip. I must be prepared to make this journey. Sometimes it seems like a trip or something that you are going through is going to take forever. And as far as eternity is concerned, that is true. However, as far as this life is concerned, things will pass. Even if it is the valley of the shadow of death, that, too, will pass. It will soon be over. I am sure everyone has heard of the saying, This, too, will pass.

The important thing is to consider what kind of trip you are going to have. No doubt many of us can remember trips. The trip itself could have been a very interesting and exciting thing. Or, it could have been a nightmare. I can remember some of both types. I remember going to the mountains, the beach, having a great trip there and fun times while there. I also remember sitting on the side of the road, car broken down, delayed flights, sleeping in the terminal, missing flights. Most of the time whether it is a "good" or "bad" trip is heavily influenced by the attitudes and behaviors of those on the trip. Sometimes it can be a result of things that we could not predict nor anticipate. But even with those unfortunate and unforeseen events, it is what you do in those circumstances that are often remembered more than the destination itself.

It is very important to know where you are headed. If you really do not have a direction, then how do you know if you have gotten there? Everyone likes to take a weekend or a day or two and just drive around. You might not have a set destination in mind. You might just be driving. But even then, you have some direction in mind. You either go right or left or straight. So, you are headed somewhere. With our lives, it is important to at least have some idea of where we want to be eventually. Otherwise, we end up going in circles and not being very productive at all.

Every journey begins at the start. You have to start. Then you can begin to manage where you are going. You can determine how fast you are going. You can see if you are making any progress. But, you have to actually begin.

Of course, with eternity in mind, where is your journey taking you? Are you headed towards heaven or hell? You are headed in one direction or the other. Which one is it for you? You can say, well, I hope I am headed to heaven. Then, you probably aren't. You can know whether or not you are headed to heaven. It is not something that you have to hope for or wonder about. You can know. How? If your faith and trust is in Christ alone, then you are on your way. If not, then you are headed in the other direction.

Where are you going? We ask that question to someone when we are not sure where they are going? We need to ask ourselves that question as well. Sometimes we are going somewhere, but we are not sure where that is. We need to stop and ask, Where am I going?

Life is a journey that we take. We are all on a pilgrimage headed somewhere. What kind of journey is it going to be and where will we end up on our journey? Those are questions that are essential to be asked and answered. We start this journey at conception. The Bible says that we are fearfully and wonderfully made, knit together, within our mother's womb. From conception to birth is around ten months. That is all part of the pilgrimage. In a sense, we are headed from the womb of our mother to the outside world. Once we have entered into the world, the pilgrimage continues. We live, grow up, perhaps marry, have our own children, grow old, and then die. Through it all, it is a journey, a pilgrimage.

My life is like a pilgrimage

A journey of twists and turns

An ever winding road

Of lessons I must learn

Though some bumps may hurt

Others bring me joy

Unexpected things come my way

That I must deploy

I traverse valleys and mountains

Rivers and peaks

I'll keep going, never tiring

No mater what life seeks

I'll keep growing and learning

From each step I take

My life is like a pilgrimage

A journey I must make - Anonymous

A Swift Post

The Bible refers to our life as a swift post. Job 9:25 answers, "Now my days are swifter than

a post: they flee away, they see no good."

A swift post has to do with a letter being delivered. The postal service takes great pride and care in trying to get that letter to its intended recipient as quickly as possible. Of course, in the 21st Century, we have instant tweets, emails, instagrams, etc. We can push a button and whatever it is that we wanted to post is out there for the world to see in a moment.

These swift posts or letters would tell of sickness, sin, death, or crime.

Before the use of horses, a runner would set out to go from one town or metropolis to the next. When they reached the town, then another runner would be ready to take the news, whatever it was, and go on to the next town, and it would repeat and so on. The same thing happened when people started using horses. A rider would ride from one town to the next and pass the mail (information, news) to a rider waiting, and so on. They were always passing along information, news. A runner- who passed along news. What is the news you are passing along? Is it good news? Is it the Good News? Are we more eager to pass along bad information than we are good information? Do we enjoy getting the juicy gossip to be able to spread to others?

Through history, mankind has used a variety of instruments to communicate with: drums, smoke signals, trumpet, letters, runners, and riders.

In this country we have seen the stage coach delivery, the pony express, trains, telegraphs, the U.S. Postal Service. We now have overnight air express, email, instant message, twitter, and probably a lot more that we haven't seen as yet.

When we write someone a letter, we think about what we are going to say. If our life is like a letter, what are you saying in your letter? What are you writing? Is it a good thing that someone will have to remember you by or something you would prefer they got rid of? What message are you sending? Who is the intended target or audience? What are you saying in your message? What are you communicating?

To whom are you writing? I am constantly writing letters to my wife and children. These are actual physical letters. But they are also letters that are being written by the way I live my life, the way I treat them, the way I lead them, the way I speak to them. I have been writing letters to my parents from the time I was born. I have been writing letters to my siblings, cousins, and extended members of the family. I write letters to my neighbors, even if I do not know them, I am still sending them a letter by how I live around them, whether or not I have ever spoken to them, and what kind of neighbor have I been. I write letters to my co-workers. I am writing letters to God. The key is what am I saying in these letters? What kind of message am I sending?

Every day you are writing letters, what are they saying?

My life is like a swift post

A journey through rocky terrain

With obstacles that often seem daunting

And goals I'm always chasing after

I trust to keep a steady pace

Amidst the chaos and the strain

That comes with life's relentless race

And the ever-changing terrain

Sometimes I feel my feet stumble

As I go through this life's test

But I push through the difficulties

To reach the promised rest

My life is like a swift post

It's a long and winding course

Though the journey is hard at times

I'm thankful for the course

For it's the trials and tribulations

That help me to stay strong

And to keep up the steady pace

As I carry on my journey along- Anonymous

A Weaver's Shuttle

James 4:14 asks, "What is your life?" Job 7:6 answers, "My days are swifter than a weaver's shuttle, and come to an end without hope."

Isaiah 38:12 states, "...As a weaver I rolled up my life. He cuts me off from the loom; From day until night You make an end of me."

When I think of the weaver's shuttle, I think of something moving really fast. So fast, that it is hard for me to keep up. That reminds me of my life sometimes. I can't keep up like I used to. I try, but the body tells me, sometimes very loudly, that I am not as young as I used to be.

Time truly goes seem to go by quickly. It seems like yesterday that I was a kid going to camp, playing ball, running around with friends. But it was actually quite a while ago. I look at young people today and think they are so young. I can't believe that students I have known for so many years are actually grown up, driving cars, going to college.

Time goes by so quickly that sometimes you just don't see it. You look around and think what happened to the time. How did this happen so quickly?

Time is something that we cannot keep. No matter how hard we try, the next second goes off the clock. We also cannot take away any time. As much as we might like to hurry things along, time is still going to go one second at a time. The weaver's shuttle goes faster than the eye. You can try to keep up with it with your eyes, but it is nearly impossible.

A lot of things can be made from the yarn that comes from a weaver's shuttle. The same thing is true with your life. You can pursue a lot of different paths, careers, relationships, and putting to use your talents and abilities. In your life, you will make a lot of things. What are you making is the question? What is the quality of what you are making? Is it good material? Will it stand the test of time?

As we live, we will undoubtedly have a lot of wear and tear. Our bodies will get older and worn out. My concern is not that will I be successful, but will I be successful at something that does not matter.

I never quite understood why some would spin the tires on their vehicle. Sometimes they would spin so fast that smoke would be pouring out of the tire and pavement. I never quite got it. I guess there is something exciting about it or they would not do it. But they never actually went anywhere. They were just spinning their tires. I want to make sure that does not happen in my life. I actually want to be headed somewhere. I do not want to be sitting and not getting anywhere.

I remember when I was a kid that we would get on the merry go round. We would try to make it go as fast as possible. Sometimes it seemed like it was going too fast, and we just wanted it to stop so we could get off. Our lives can seem like they are spinning out of control. You can't seem to stop it or even slow it down. While sitting on the merry go round it obviously seems like you are spinning round and round. We say that something makes our head spin. Sometimes life seems that way, that it is spinning and we have no control.

While we are living, every day, like the shuttle, we leave threads behind. But if, while we live, we live unto the Lord, in works of faith and labours of love, we shall have the benefit, for every man shall reap as he sowed, and wear as he wove.

They are short and few. He does not here refer so much to the rapidity with which they were passing away as to the fact that they would soon be gone, and that he was likely to be cut off without being permitted to enjoy the blessings of a long life. The weaver's shuttle is the instrument by which the weaver inserts the filling in the wool. With us few things would furnish a more striking emblem of rapidity than the speed with which a weaver throws his shuttle from one side of the web to the other. It would seem that such was the fact among the ancients, though the precise manner in which they wove their cloth, is unknown. It was common to compare life with a web, which was filled up by the successive days. The ancient Classical writers spoke of it as a web woven by the Fates. We can all feel the force of the comparison used here by Job, that the days which we live fly swift away. How rapidly is one after another added to the web of life. How soon will the whole web be filled up, and life be closed. A few more shoots of the shuttle and all will be over, and our life will be cut off, as the weaver removes one web from the loom to make way for another. How important to improve the fleeting moments, and to live as if we were soon to see the rapid shuttle flying for the last time. A weaver's shuttle, by means of which the web is shot between the threads of the warp as they are drawn up and down. His days pass as swiftly by as the little shuttle passes backwards and forwards in the warp.

My life is like a weaver's shuttle,

It moves up and down and back and forth,

Weaving a tapestry of days and moments,

Creating a beauty of its own course.

Sometimes it moves swiftly,

Sometimes it lingers a while,

Traveling to many places and faces,

Not always knowing which way to go.

But like the weaver, I too, have a plan,

A plan unseen, but known in my heart,

I keep weaving, and reweaving,

My tapestry of life.
It's one of joy and pain,

Of laughter and tears,

Of highs and lows,

Of darkness and light.

My life is like a weaver's shuttle,

Travelling through this life,

I keep weaving, and reweaving,

My tapestry of life. -Anonymous

A Swift Ship

James 4:14 asks, "What is your life?" Job 9:26

anwers, "They are passed away as the swift ships…"

I can remember being at the beach and watching

ships out in the distance. At first they appeared to be

moving very slowly, but as I kept looking up at them I

would notice how they were moving further along in the

horizon until they were finally out of sight. I have been on

a sailboat and when the wind picks up, they can really start moving quite fast. Of course, if you are rowing or have a motor on the boat, they could move even faster. That is the comparison that is made to our lives. Our lives are like these swift boats moving across the horizon of the ocean until at last they are gone. Those that are lightest built and run swiftest.

Being on a boat is a lot of fun. It is great to be out on the water and enjoying the sun, wind, and water. You can take your time and be at leisure while being out on the boat. It can take you a lot of places depending on where you want to go. That is a tremendous question, where do you want to go?

Ships carry a variety of cargo. They can carry people, food, military equipment, vehicles, planes, etc. There are ships that are set just to provide entertainment.

Ships move across the horizon but leave no trace or track behind them. They leave a wake but that is soon gone. This is a great picture of our lives as well. At times it seems as if it is moving very slowly. Other times, it appears to be moving too quickly. Eventually, it moves completely out of the picture.

There is something special about sailing. You can let the wind take you as fast and as far as it can. Most sailboats have a motor for emergencies or if there is no wind. The sails fill out and flap in the wind. It is very peaceful and relaxing.

If the wind dies down, the boat can simply drift in the current. If you are on a lake, you will probably eventually drift to the shore. If you are on a river, the current can take you a far distance in a short amount of time. You might go into the shoreline but it will usually be a good distance down the river. If you are on the ocean, the waves can take you further away from the shoreline.

Unless you drop an anchor, you will probably drift from where you are. Your life can be like that at times. You lose your anchor or mooring. You begin to drift with no direction or purpose. It is hard to tell where you will end up. It is usually a long ways away from where you wanted to be or expected to be.

Who is the head of your ship? There can only be one captain of the ship. There is one person who makes the decisions. Who is making the decisions in your life? Who is the captain of your ship? It can be you. But then you have to know where you are going, how to get there, and how to manage all of the obstacles you face along the way. If God is the Captain, then, we can set back and enjoy the ride. We simply do what the Captain tells us to do. The experience is more peaceful and much easier.

At a distance the ship does not seem like it is moving very fast. It slowly slips out of sight. The ship is always moving in a direction. What direction are you headed?

Every ship needs an anchor. Without the anchor could be adrift. Are you drifting away? It does not take long to be far away. What is our anchor? Our anchor should be the Word of God and our faith. Knowing and trusting in His Word and the promise of salvation for those who put their faith in Christ, should provide a solid anchor for all believers.

You need a compass to show you the way. What is our compass? The Bible is our compass. It shows us the way. Psalm 119:105 states, "Thy word is a lamp unto my feet and a light unto my path." If we lose our compass, we might not know which way to go. If we do not follow the Word, we can certainly lose our way. How are we to know what to do next, where to go, how to get there, etc.,?

The last thing you want to happen while on a boat is for it to start taking on water. Hopefully you have a pump to get rid of the water. If not, eventually it will sink. The same is true with our lives. If we take on too much water we will sink. Our relationships will sink. Our businesses will sink.

This ship has sailed is a phrase meaning that time has passed on this particular opportunity or event. It is too late. As far as life is concerned, we only get one ship. There is not another one which will come along later. We do not want to waste time or miss out on opportunities. We do not want our ship of life to sail on us and we miss it.

My life is like a swift moving ship,

Heading to new shores and unknown trips,

Onward I journey to unseen places,

Discovering new sights, faces and cases.

I navigate the choppy waves,

My faith and courage, my will to be brave.

Dodging and weaving, making my own way,

Moving ever forward, never delay.

Dashing through the deep blue sea,

My life is an adventure of joy and glee.

Sometimes the waters are clam and clear,

Other times I face obstacles and fear.

Though I'm often battered and bruised,

I remain unbowed and will not be used.

My life is a swift moving ship,

Heading to new shores and unknown trips. - Anonymous

A Handbreadth

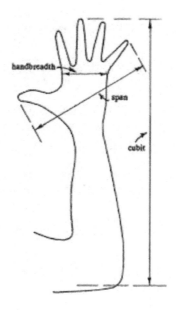

James 4:14 asks, "What is your life?" Psalms 39:5 answers, "Behold, thou hast made my days as a handbreadth; and mine age is as nothing before thee: verily every man at his best state is altogether vanity. Selah."

A hand-breath is the length from the top of your thumb to the top of your little finger or pinkie finger when the hand is outstretched. Compared to the length of a life, it does not seem that long. The length of your life, even if you live eighty to ninety years compared to eternity does not see long at all.

What are all the things we do with our hands, specifically the length of the hand? One thing that we do is to use our hands to work. Whether I am typing a letter, driving a vehicle, laying blocks, or using a saw or any other tool, the hands are needed to perform work. Most of what we do is only for this life. This is needed as we provide for our families and do the work that is set before us. All of our work should be done for the glory of the Lord. We should also consider what is going to last for eternity. Those are the things that really matter the most. What is done for Christ will last.

We can also use our hands for encouragement. We can clap for someone when they have done something or accomplished something. When someone sings or plays an instrument or makes a shot, etc., we can clap our hands together to show our encouragement and approval. We can also clap when someone has done their best but perhaps did not win the contest or match. They still deserve a hand clap because they did their very best. We can also pat someone on the back or shoulder indicating our approval and appreciation. It is amazing what something as simple as a pat on the back does for someone's self esteem or feeling encouraged. Often times it is exactly what they needed. And it is something that we can do which requires very little effort on our part. It does not take much to pat someone on the back.

A handshake welcomes someone. It also shows friendship or being open to meeting someone. It can also be used to express thanks. We can use our hands to give a hug. This shows affection and love. Parents will often hold their children's hand. Spouses will show affection and intimacy by holding hands with each other. Two people dating might hold hands to show that they are together and in a relationship.

We use our hands in worship. We might lift one or both of our hands towards the heavens, towards the Lord in worship. We might fold our hands to pray. The old children's song states, "Be careful little hands what you do." The following is a list of some of the passages of Scripture which tell us to lift up our hands in worship.

I Timothy 2:8 "I desire therefore that the men pray everywhere, lifting up holy hands, without wrath and doubting."

I Kings 8:22 "Then Solomon stood before the altar of the Lord in the presence of all the assembly of Israel and spread out his hands toward heaven."

I Kings 8:54 "And so it was, when Solomon had finished praying all this prayer and supplication to the Lord, that he arose from before the altar of the Lord, from kneeling on his knees with his hands spread up to heaven."

Nehemiah 8:6 "And Ezra blessed the Lord, the great God. Then all the people answered, Amen, Amen! While lifting up their hands. And they bowed their heads and worshiped the Lord with their faces to the ground."

Psalm 63:4 "Thus I will bless You while I live; I will lift up my hands in Your name."

Psalm 119:48 "My hands also I will lift up to Your commandments, which I love, and I will meditate on Your statutes."

Psalm 28:2 "Hear the voice of my supplications when I cry to You, when I lift up my hands toward Your holy sanctuary."

Psalm 141:2 "Let my prayer be set before You as incense, the lifting up of my hands as the evening sacrifice."

Psalm 134:2 "Lift up your hands in the sanctuary, and bless the Lord."

Lamentations 2:19 "Arise, cry out in the night at the beginning of the watches; pour out your heart like water before the face of the Lord. Lift your hands toward Him for the life of your young children, who faint from hunger at the head of every street."

Lamentations 3:41 "Let us lift our hearts and hands to God in heaven."

Ezra 9:5 "And at the evening sacrifice I arose up from my heaviness; and having rent my garment and my mantle, I fell upon my knees, and spread out my hands unto the Lord my God."

Daniel 12:7 "And I heard the man clothed in linen, which was upon the waters of the river, when he held up his right hand and his left hand unto heaven, and sware by him that liveth for ever that is shall be for a time, times, and an half; and when he shall have accomplished to scatter the power of the holy people, all these things shall be finished."

My life is like a handbreath,

It's barely there, but it's everything.

It's filled with moment of joy and sorrow,

With days of laughter and of tears.

It's the little things that make me smile,

The moments that make me laugh.

The memories that linger in my soul,

And the people that I love.

It's the simply moments of beauty,

The moment that I cherish.

The moments that take my breath away

And the ones that I will never forget.

It's the moments that I want to make count,

The moments that I want to savor.

The moments that I want to remember,

The moments that give me strength.

My life is like a handbreath,

It's barely there, but it's everything.

It's filled with moments of beauty and love,

And I wouldn't trade it for the world. - Anonymous

As a Shepherd's Tent Removed

James 4:14 asks, "What is your life?" Isaiah 38:12

answers, "Like a shepherd's tent my

dwelling is pulled up and removed from me…"

The Israelites would certainly have understood the

illustration of a shepherd's tent being compared to

something that did not last long. As many of them were

nomads, especially those that wandered in the wilderness

for forty years, they moved a lot. As soon as the grass was

gone so were they. They became proficient in putting the

tent up and taking it down quickly. That is certainly not something that I ever mastered. I can remember when the children were younger that we did the whole tenting out thing. Setting up the tent, which was supposed to be easy and only thirty minutes, usually took a wee bit longer.

The Scripture refers to God's people as being pilgrims, sojourners in a land that is only temporary. Maybe that is why they used tents so much. A tent is normally a temporary thing. If we go camping, we usually do not plan on staying permanently. Even refugees who find themselves in refugee camps, hope to only be there for a while. The same is true with our stay on Earth. Even if we live a hundred years, that is only temporary compared to eternity in heaven.

While there is nothing wrong with wanting a nice home, and we are certainly to be good steward of what God has given to us, our homes here are only temporary dwellings. We will soon pass, and those homes will be for someone else.

Recreational Vehicles are definitely a step up from tents. However, they, too, are supposed to be temporary. Some people buy larger ones and live in them instead of regular houses. They like the flexibility of being able to move around. But that is the exception not the rule. If we have an R.V. at a camp site, we will use it as we have vacation time or on the weekends. Normally, we are not in it all of the time.

RVers and tenters come into a campground or an area, put up their tents or hook up their rvs, stay as long as they plan on staying and then they are gone. They might do a lot of activities while they are there or they might just rest, sleep and relax. Some will only stay a night, while others might stay a week or even a month. However, eventually, they leave. The same is true for our lives. There might be a lot of activities that go on while we are here.

Some of us stay longer than others. But, we all eventually leave.

There certainly might be advantages to going tenting. You often have great views. Many people like the idea that for the most part you are left alone. It is quiet and peaceful. And, it is always changing.

It is important to make sure that you anchor the tent down. Otherwise you might be chasing it or trying to put it back up when a gust of wind picks up. We must make sure we are anchored spiritually as well. When the storms of life come, and they will come, if we do not have an anchor, we will be blown around to and fro. Depending on the size of the storm and the strength of the wind, your life could be devastated.

It is important that we are careful where you put our tent. Location, location, location, is the old saying. You do not want to put it on top of a bees nest, or on a slope, or a number of other bad locations. I knew someone once who put their tent over the sprinkler which promptly came up the next morning and gave them a surprise. Lot placed his tent looking toward Sodom and Gomorrah. We find that when the angels come to destroy the cities, that Lot was now living right in the midst of the degradation. Where is our life headed? What is it pointed towards? That is the thing about being pointed in a certain direction, you usually end up there sooner or later.

When you go tenting, you want to make sure that you have the supplies that you will need. The supplies usually depend on where you are going, the time of year, and how long you are planning on staying. If you are going where it will be colder, then appropriate clothes and bedding will be needed. The longer you plan on staying the more supplies you will need. We eventually will be spending eternity somewhere. The provisions that we need to acquire is a relationship with Christ. They will determine our ultimate and final destination.

One thing that every tenter will learn is that you don't leave the door wide open while you are gone. You want to zip up the tent while you are away to prevent any unwanted critters from moving in. When it is time to go in for a nap or bedtime, the last thing you want to find is that you are now sharing your space with a snake, skunk, or other unwanted animal. Protect your life, your spiritual person as well. There will be a constant flow of unwanted people trying to get into your life. They are not there to make your life or stay more pleasant. They are there to make your life miserable and create as much strife as possible. Zip up those tents.

Tents use to have a main pole right in the middle of the tent to help keep the rest of it up. One thing that you always wanted to make sure you didn't do was to knock down the pole. If you did, then the entire tent was in danger of coming down. The same thing is true with our lives. What is holding you up? What is your main support? You want to make sure you do not knock that down. Protect what is holding you up.

My life is like a shepherd's tent removed

From place to place, I too shall roam

The wilderness my home,

I'm not averse to trod a rugged, thankless course

Though sometimes I may feel forlorn

I always keep my faith reborn

From day to day, I still persist

To make my life a thing of bliss

My hopes, my dreams, my faith, my love

Are all that I shall ever need

To help me move from spot to spot

And fill my life with joy and peace

Like a shepherd's tent that is moved around

My life is ever shifting ground

My joys, my sorrows, my highs, my lows

Are marked by changes that I chose

Though I may never stay in one place too long

I'm never without song or grace

For I know that in this life of mine

I'm blessed with a sheltering tent of time. - Anonymous

As a Weaver's Thread Cut

James 4:14 asks, "What is your life?" Isaiah 38:12

answers, "…I have cut off like a

weaver my life…"

The weaver will cut the thread. The scissors or the

knife goes through it as if it is nothing. In an instant it is

cut. This is why the comparison is made to life. In an

instant it is gone. We live our lives, however long that will

be, but we die in an instant.

The thread of life is delicate and tender. We have to be careful with the thread. It needs to be handled gently.

There is a saying that we or something might be "hanging by a thread." It is precariously close to breaking. Our life is always precariously close to the end. In fact, we are only one step away from death. We never know when that will be.

We might also say that we are at the end of our rope. This means that we don't think we can take any more or endure any more than what we are enduring.

Frayed ends on clothes will unravel. If they are not cut off, they will get worse. Sometimes we might say that someone looks frayed, meaning they look really tired or overwhelmed by something. We can become frayed at the ends, spiritually, physically, psychologically, socially, etc.

Sometimes we say that we are tied up and cannot do something or get to something or come to something. What has us tied up? What is keeping us from doing what we are supposed to be doing? Is there any thread that needs to be cut so that we are not tied up as much? Do we spend enough time with our families? Are we in God's Word like we should be, or, are we tied up?

There is a song we use to sing at camp, I am wrapped up, tied up and tangled up in Jesus. Jesus is my all in all. If we are going to be tied up, it should be by the Lord and His Word.

My life is like a weaver's thread,

Cut suddenly and left unsaid.

It's spun not knowing where it will lead,

But it can be unraveled and mended with speed.

It's a pattern of twists and turns,

Changes and lessons that I must learn.

Sorrows and joys, both come in time,

Each one lasting for a certain rhyme.

The threads of my life are ever changing,

Never in one place, always rearranging.

The pattern of my life is ever shifting,

I must keep up, never drifting.

Though sometimes I'm cut off too soon,

I can pick up the pieces and make a new loom.

My life is like a weaver's thread,

Cut suddenly but mended with speed. - Anonymous

A Dream

James 4:14 asks, "What is your life?" Job 20:8 answers, "He shall fly away as a dream, and shall not be found: yea, he shall be chased away as a vision of the night."

Probably most of us if not all of us have had a dream at some point in life. Some dreams are nice, and when we wake up, we might try to go back to sleep so to get back into that dream. But that seldom happens. Usually it is gone, not to come back. It is over quickly and then you have a hard time remembering. We try to go back to sleep and finish your dream but to no avail.

Sometimes dreams can seem like a mixture, part dream, part real life. I might ask if I was dreaming or was that real? We often dream about what has happened. It is a way of remembering the past. But sometimes we dream about what is going to happen. Then, when that event actually takes place, we are amazed and wondering like deja vu.

We know that God uses dreams. There are many examples of God or through angels, God sending a message to someone in a dream. In Genesis 20 we find that God stops Abimelech, the king of Gerar, from sleeping with Sarah, Abraham's wife. In Genesis 28:12, Jacob sees angels ascending and descending a ladder between earth and heaven. In Genesis 31:10-11, the Lord tells Jacob to return to the land of his father. In Genesis 31:24, God warns Laban not to bless or curse Jacob as he heads home. Genesis 37:1-10 shows Joseph's dream about grain and stars. One sheaf stands straight up; eleven others bow to it. The sun, moon, and stars bow down to Joseph. Both dreams signify that Joseph's family will bow to him.

In Genesis 40, we find dreams that Joseph interprets. There are three branches. The cupbearer presses grapes from a vine and gives them to Pharoah. There are three baskets. The baker carriers three baskets of bread on his head, and the birds eat it. Both dreams signify these men's fates after three days. The cupbearer is restored to honor. The baker is executed. There are two dreams in Genesis 41 that Pharoah wants interpreted. The first one is Pharoah's cows. Seven fat cows come up from the Nile to graze, but seven thin cows devour the fat cows. The second one is Pharoah's stalk. Seven plump ears of grain grow on a single stalk, but seven thin ears swallow them. Both dreams signify that Egypt will undergo seven years of plenty and then seven years of famine. In Judges 7:13 an unnamed man has a dream about a piece of bread that rolls into the camp of the Midianites and turns over the tents. This foretells Gideon's victory. In I Kings 3:5-15, the Lord appears to Solomon, the new king of Israel, and offers him anything. Solomon chooses wisdom.

Nebuchadnezzar has a dream in Daniel 2. A great statute made of various materials which symbolize future empires is crushed by a stone which symbolizes the Kingdom of God.

Nebuchadnezzar has another dream in Daniel 4. He dreams of an enormous tree that is hacked to the earth. This symbolizes Nebuchadnezzar's future seven years of insanity.

In Daniel 7 we find a dream of a lion, bear, leopard, and a mysterious beast with ten horns who are all judged by

God. The Son of Man is given dominion. The beasts represent the four kingdoms.

In Matthew 1:18-24 an angel tells Joseph (the carpenter) not to divorce Mary: her child is the Savior. There were four dreams given to protect the young Christ child. The Magi's warning was a dream warning the Magi not to return to Herod when they left Bethlehem. An angel tells Joseph in a dream to escape before Herod kills all the male babies. An angel tells Joseph that it is safe to return to Israel with Jesus because Herod had died. Since Herod's son was on the throne in Judea, God warns Joseph to not go to Judea, so he goes to Nazareth.

In Matthew 27:19, Pontius Pilate's wife has a nightmare concerning the trial of Jesus because she knows he is innocent She warns her husband not to have anything to do with him.

In regards to end times, Acts 2:17 states, "And it shall come to pass in the last days, saith God, I will pour out of my Spirit upon all flesh: and your sons and your daughters shall prophesy, and your young men shall see visions, and your old men shall dream dreams."

Not every dream is from God. Anything that is contrary to the Word of God and the Holy Spirit's working within your life, is not from God. God does not contradict Himself nor will He tell you to do something in a dream that He has forbidden in His Word.

We also talk about dreams by means of a hope or plan. Dream big we are often told. And, it is possible, that we concentrate so much on our dreams that they enter into our sleep time by way of a dream. But the reality is that we can't just dream. We have to work to make it reality. It doesn't just happen to us. We have to make it happen. If you are going to dream, dream big.

My life is like a dream that is soon gone,

A fleeting thought that won't linger long.

A misty morning that fades away

A fleeting moment that fades to gray.

A passing moment that slips away,

A twinkle of stars that will soon be gone,

A dream that I wish would remain,

A feeling that will never stay.

A time that will never come again,

A beauty that I can no longer see,

A moment that is gone too soon,

A dream that will never be.

My life is like a dream that is soon gone,

A fleeting thought that won't linger long,

A passing moment that slips away,

A dream that I wish would remain. - Anonymous

A Sleep

James 4:14 asks, "What is your life?" Psalms 90:5 answers, "You carry them away like a flood; they are like a sleep. In the morning they are like grass which grows up."

We all know that sleep does not last long. Often we fall asleep and then the alarm goes off what seems like only minutes afterward. We can question the timing. It can't be 6 o'clock already might be something a lot of people say.

You can adjust the actual time for whatever fits you the best. But the fact is that we are seldom ready for the time to get up. It passes by so quickly. We are not ready for it to be over. The same is often true with life. We are not ready for it to be over whether for ourselves or for someone else. It seems to have gone by too quickly.

We often wish we had more time to sleep. If I could just get another thirty minutes or sleep in a little this morning. We might have our snooze set for ten more minutes. If I could just have ten more minutes. The same might be true for life when it comes down to the end. We might wish we could have a little longer. The important thing is to make sure we use what we have in the best way possible.

There is only so much time to sleep and then sleep is over and we have to get up and go. The same is true with life. There is only so much time we have in life. Then it will be over and we have to get up and go.

We need rest so we can be refreshed. The Sabbath rest is a biblical principle and precedent. The Lord rested on the seventh day. While on Earth, we find that Jesus goes and rests and takes the disciples to rest. But they did not rest their life away, they got what was needed, but then used the refreshing to be about the Father's business.

One day we will enter into eternal rest, but until then, we must rest so that we can return to the task the Lord has given us to do.

My life is like a sleep that soon passes

A fleeting moment that I must seize

For in the blink of an eye it is gone

Leaving me to reminisce

Though I may take for granted each day

I know that I must seize my chance

To make the most of my life's journey

And to take part in its dance

The days may seem so fleeting

And the night may seem so long

But I must take the time to savor

All the moments of this song

For life is like a sheep that soon passes

But it can be filled with joy and peace

But I must seize each moment

For it will never come again, at least - Anonymous

A Vapor

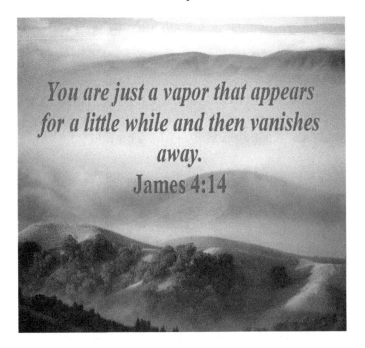

James 4:14 states, "You are just a vapor that appears for a little while and then vanishes away."

A vapor is very temporary. We see it for a moment and then it is gone. Where did it go? It vanishes so quickly. You saw it. You know it was there. But now it is gone. You can see it in a valley as fog. Sometimes at the top of the mountain it is dense for a little while, and then begins to disappear.

There are times when you can walk down in a valley and see the mist or fog all around you. It can seem to be thick even though it is just a mist. Suddenly, it begins to disappear. It is hard to know where it goes, it just evaporates and is gone. This is life. You find yourself in the midst of it and suddenly it begins to disappear. Where did it go? It is hard to say. You know it was there, but then it is not. You might try to hold on to it, but it is impossible. It slips right through your fingers.

Fog can be very thick at times. When you are driving, you have to slow down because you cannot see very far in front of you. You have to keep your eyes focused and your hands on the wheel. This can be the way life is at times. You have to stay focused on what is happening in front of you. You have to keep both hands on the wheel. Then, suddenly, you begin to drive through it. The fog begins to lift and eventually is gone. You can relax a little because the driving is not as intense. This is life.

Sometimes you have to slow down and focus on the specific thing you are experiencing at the time. Then, before you know it, you have driven through it. You are on the other side and things look clearer and brighter.

Some of the heaviest fog comes with the changing of seasons. It is still cold but trying to get warmer. Warm air pushes in overhead and colder air is still on the ground perhaps because of snow or ice still there. Or, the warm summer air is still present but the colder air begins to push it out of the way. Some of the most difficult times for us in our lives is when there is a change of season in our life. This could be a variety of things including getting married, having children, graduating from high school or college. It could also be losing a job, losing a loved one, or getting older and not able to do the things you used to do. We might find that this week there is a lot of heavy fog. This specific time of life requires me to slow down and concentrate on one thing at a time.

Most of the time, we like to be able to see way down the road. We do not want any surprises or suddenly come upon something we did not see coming. We do not like it when we can't see too far in front of us. Most of life is this way. It is really hard to see way down the road. There are a lot of twists and turns, mountains and valleys, bad weather, fog. This causes us to have to slow down. Perhaps we would not ever slow down if we were not forced to do so.

When it is foggy on the road, you have to keep your eyes open. You cannot day dream or take your eyes off the road. If you do so, you might come upon another vehicle, a turn in the road, or a stop sign. You cannot afford to take a chance. In life, we need to keep our eyes open and observe the people and things around us. As we observe we can often see the circumstances behind what people are doing or saying. It gives us a better perspective. We are tuned in to everything that is happening. It causes us to have to pay close attention.

I do not know if you have ever been walking in fog or mist. You can feel the wetness of the water vapors, but you really can't get a hold on it. You can try to grab a handful of the fog, but it will simply disappear in your hands. It seems like life is like that at times. You just can't get a handle on it. You would like to grasp it, but it slips right thru your fingers. Instead of trying to hold on to it, perhaps it is better to simply walk through it, live it, experience it. You cannot grab it and put it in a container to open up later on. This day, this experience, this moment, is to be experienced right now. It will soon be gone not to return.

There is nothing we can do to stop it from going away. The fog comes and goes and we cannot do anything about its arrival or departure. The only thing we can do is to experience it while it is here. This is true of others in our lives. They arrive and depart, and we cannot control either end of that. All we can do is enjoy the time we have and the experiences we share. We need to stop wasting our time on trying to do something we will never be able to do. Instead, concentrate on what you can do.

There have been times I have been driving or walking through the fog and it seems as it I have been engulfed with the vapors. I cannot see two feet in front of me, and all around me is this thick fog. You might seem engulfed by life at times. It can be heavy decisions, terrible events, or heartbreaking news. Life has you on all sides, and you cannot see to make the next step. Sometimes you have to wait. Turn on your flashers and pull off the road. Stand still and wait for the fog to lighten and then disappear. Waiting is difficult, but sometimes absolutely necessary.

Even thou eighty years seems like a long time to live we are warned about taking it for granted. Compared to eternity, eighty years is but a moment. Sometimes we forget that every day is a gift not a guarantee. We need to consider if the plans we are making are pleasing to God. We must make time to serve others.

A vapor cannot make its existence last any longer than it is going to last. We cannot gain one second more than what our lives are going to be. We need to redeem the time and enjoy the moment we are in.

My life is like a vapor, so fleeting and so swift

A passing moment that's gone before I can lift

A single finger, a single thought, a single breath

A single moment of joy I can never forget

A life that is so precious, so short and so brief

A life that can be taken away in a thief

A single moment of sorrow, a single tear of pain

A single moment of sadness that will remain

My life is like a vapor, it passes so quickly

A single moment of life that I can never keep

A single moment of joy, a single moment of bliss

A single moment of hope that I can never miss

My like is like a vapor, so unpredictable and wild

A single moment of courage that I must keep in mind

A single moment of courage that I need to find

A single moment of strength that will help me climb

My like is like a vapor, so precious and so brief

A single moment of life that I must not forget

A single moment of joy, a single moment of bliss

A single moment of life that I must never miss. -
Anonymous

A Shadow

James 4:14 asks, "What is your life?" I Chronicles 29:15 answers, "For we are aliens and pilgrims before You, as were all our fathers; our days on earth are as a shadow, and without hope."

This verse reminds us of the frailty and shortness of life. Man's days are fleeing away that the shadow flees away. The shadow declines and then is gone.

A shadow is something interesting. The sun or a light provides the shadow from not only us, but from others and other objects. But just as soon as the sun fades or moves, so does the shadow. As soon as you take a step, the shadow moves or is gone. The is a comparison to our lives. It seems like just a step or two and it has passed.

Your shadow is always with you. You might not always see it, but it is there ready to extend itself. It is a constant companion waiting to be seen. We often take for granted our life, the breath of life, health of life, until they are gone. It is right there with you until it is not.

There is an old saying that someone is afraid of their shadow. It indicates that they are afraid of just about everything. It is interesting that horses are afraid of shadows including their own. They will sometimes spook when they see it because they do not know what it is.

Your shadow always follows you. Just like your shadow walks with you so life and death walk together. Death is always lurking waiting for its time. It will only be when we are in eternal life that we will no longer have death as a constant companion.

If there is no light, there is no shadow. It is just darkness. The shadow needs a light to be seen.

I do not know if you have ever tried to catch your shadow or get ahead of it. It is an impossible task. You will never catch up to it. It is always a step ahead of you.

There will be no shadows in heaven. There will be no darkness. Jesus Himself will be the light of heaven.

There is a direct relation from the shadow to the sun. There is also a direct relation from our lives to the Son, the Son of God.

When the Sun goes down the shadows flee.

My life is like a shadow,

That follows me around,

It's ever-changing,

Never quite the same

It comes and goes without sound.

Sometimes it's strong and bright,

Filling me with a drive,

A passion and a purpose,

A spark that's sure to thrive.

Other times it's faint and dim,

Hiding me in the shade,

A feeling of despair,

A journey left unmade.

But no matter what the shape,

My life is like a shadow,

It's always there for me,

To bring me joy, fear, and sorrow. -Anonymous

A Flower

James 4:14 asks, "What is your life?" Isaiah 40:6-7 answers, "The voice said, 'Cry out!' And he said, 'What shall I cry?' 'All flesh is grass, and all its loveliness is like the flower of the field. The grass withers, the flower fades, because the breath of the Lord blows upon it; surely the people are grass.'"

I love flowers. I like to see what kind of flower is going to come forth. I like the different colors and smells. It is pretty to see the blossoms come forth. It blooms, but the blooms fade. Eventually the flower will fade and wilt away. The blossoms will grow old and fall off.

Just like the flower is pretty, so is life. At least some parts of life are beautiful. The birth of a child. Love. Relationships. Connections. Friendships. Sunsets. Sunrises. Picturesque landscapes. Breathtaking views. I am sure you can add others as well. But all of these eventually go away or fade.

We might see a flower or an arrangement of flowers and say that they are nice. That's nice. I am sure that there are many times in life that certain things happen that we would refer to as, That's nice. But these events become memories. We can think back on them and reminisce. But they are back there, in the past. So, is our life. Memories, but memories are in the past.

Just as quickly as the flower came forth and bloomed, it is gone. It impacted those who saw it and interacted with it. It left an impression. But it is still gone.

Beauty does not last. We can take a picture or paint one and put it on the wall. However, the object or person that we are photographing will grow old and not be as young and vibrant as before.

Strength does not last. The flower stands strong for a time. But as it withers, so does its strength. And before long, it will wilt and bend over. Our strength will not last. Even if we try our best to stay in shape, lose weight, stay healthy, etc., eventually our strength will wane.

Health does not last. The healthiest person in the world will one day die. Eventually everyone's body will wear out. Organs will stop working. The heart will slow down. It is inevitable.

Beauty fades. God does not. What was new and young will wilt and become old. It will fade in its beauty and glory.

The flower speaks of God's creation. It brings attention to Christ, the Creator.

Speaks but is silent. There are a lot of things especially in God's creation that speaks loudly but has no tongue or voice. It says no actual words.

My life is like a flower that soon fades

A beauty that I want to keep for days

But as time passes by I'm forced to face

This beauty that I have soon decays

As I bloom and blossom forth with grace

My petals are so soft and so sweet

But they eventually start to wilt

My life is like a flower that soon fades

Though I try to hold on tight

The beauty I have is not here to stay

My life is like a flower that soon fades

A beauty that I want to keep for days

So I cherish the beauty I have today

And try to make the best of what remains

For I know soon the petals will all be gone

My life is like a flower that soon fades. - Anonymous

Water Spilt on the Ground

James 4:14 asks, "What is your life?" 2 Samuel 14:14 answers, "For we will surely die and become like water spilled on the ground, which cannot be gathered up again."

The snows can be high from the winter storms. However, when spring comes and the warmer weather moves in, the snow begins to melt, and it is often rapidly. If you add to that any rain, then the snow quickly joins the running water filling the creeks and rivers. Eventually they flow into the ocean.

Water is often used to water everything from plants and flowers to trees and even humans ourselves. It is estimated that we should drink between 11 and 15 cups of water a day. As a general rule, a person can survive without water for about three days. It is essential to our well being and even our continual existence.

Are you watering anything? Is your life being used in a way to provide needed nourishment to others? Or is it simply being spilled on the ground, poured out, but for no purpose or goal?

Are you run off? Sometimes water runs off and really does not provide anything to plants or flowers. It comes down too quickly or flows too fast and does not have time to penetrate into the ground where it can find the roots and be soaked in.

Are you stagnant? Water can become stagnant and polluted if it does not continue to move. This can become true in our own lives if we become stagnant and cease to move forward. We must be moving forward with the Lord and in His Word. Otherwise, we will stagnate and not be able to be productive.

Are you attracting mosquitoes? Stagnant water will often attract mosquitoes and other forms of insects. If you are not moving forward with the Lord, you are likely to attract those things and people which would not be good for you. It is a good question to ask from time to time. What are we attracting?

Where did it go? You know it was there, but now it is gone. You could feel it, but now it

has disappeared.

Rain comes in a lot of different forms. One thing that the ground often needs is steady rain. We often refer to it as a good soaker. We do not want it to come too fast and just run off the top of the ground. We want it to sink down into the ground. It is most useful that way. We do not want our lives to simply be here and gone without any lasting effect.

Water wakes you up. You can wash your face in the morning, and it wakes you up.

Sometimes we need a little water splashed on our face to wake us up. It helps us to focus and to

see clearly.

Water cleanses. It washes away the grime and dirt. There is a reason we take a shower or

a bath. We get dirty. I do not know of anything other than water that we use to cleanse ourselves.

We do not take a shower with soda, tea, or coffee. We also want clean water as it would be of little value to take a shower with dirty water. We need our

sins washed away every day. As we

live our lives, we cannot help but get dirty by the world. It

pushes in on us and as we handle it,

touch it, it gets us dirty. Everyone needs a good cleansing.

My life is like water spilt on the ground

It moves, it ebbs, it's never quite sound

It starts off calm and quiet and serene

But sometimes it boils and churns so mean

It can be wild and carefree, it can be slow

It can be a raging river, ready to flow

It can be a raging sea, ready to roar

It can be still and placid, nothing more

Sometimes it's a torrent that rushes by

Sometimes it's a puddle, calm and dry

Sometimes it's a fountain, pure and clear

Sometimes it's a raging storm that's severe

My life is like water spilt on the ground

It moves, it ebbs, it's never quite sound

It changes, it flows, and it takes its course

But always it's there, no matter the source. - Anonymous

Grass

James 4:14 asks, "What is your life?" I Peter 1:24 answers, "All flesh is as grass, and all the glory of man as the flower of the grass. The grass withers, and its flower falls away."

I am probably no different than a lot of people who think back over their life and can say that I wasted too much time on things that really did not matter. Most of us can remember being told to not waste time. Of course, the reason is that time goes by so quickly and our lives are soon lived. We want to be able to say that we spent our lives on things that mattered.

When the young shoots burst through the ground, they have plenty of potential. While they have the opportunity and time, they are green, healthy, and to many animals, nutritious. But this only lasts for a short time and then they begin to fade and lose that tenderness. The same is true with humans. When we are young, we have so much promise, energy, and time. But that only lasts for a season. What are we going to do with the time allotted to us?

I have cut a lot of grass in my life. I cut the grass where I grew up with about a quarter of an acre for a front yard. While in college, I had a mowing business where I cut the grass of several people in the area. Then, when we moved to the camp where we served, I often cut the grass there which was several acres. I have always enjoyed cutting grass and/or hay as well. It comes up and grows, but at a certain point it needs to be cut or it will begin to lose its nutritional value.

Against the mower the grass has no chance. When it is our time to go, we will not be able to stand against it either. No matter how hard we try or what we say, when it is our time, we will go.

Animals eat it. It certainly has value. We use the animals for meat and milk. The better the grass the more nutritious it is. The animals will eat more and have better meat and/or milk.

When winter comes the grass dies down. It is still there, just dormant. It is hibernating for the cold months. There will be times when we will need to hibernate or at least take time to refresh to refuel for the next adventure or part of life. It is not dead, just resting. Waiting for springtime so that it can go back to its purpose.

There will come a time when there will be no more growth for the grass. In fact, what will happen is that it will begin to die.

Grass goes from green to brown as it dies. It withers away. After it reaches full growth, it will turn brown and begin to fade and wilt. The same is true with our earthly bodies. They will get old, deteriorate and break down. It is part of the curse of death. We wear out.

Grass needs good soil, water, and sunshine to grow. We need water, food, and a good amount of sunshine to properly grow. We also need our minds to be stimulated for mental growth. As we mature and learn to socially process things, we grow emotionally. We also need to grow spiritually. For spiritually growth, we need the Word of God, to pray, worship, and fellowship with Him and fellow believers.

What can grass do? Grass takes in the nutrients from the soil and the water from the rain. It lives and grows as long as it can. It produces the best blade of grass possible. We are to do the same. We live and grow physically, mentally, emotionally and spiritually. The grass does not worry about living or dying. It simply grows and lives until it doesn't. Live do not worry about living or dying.

My life is like the grass so green and tall,

My days they come, but they are so small.

I live in a world without much rest,

Where my life is cut down like a test.

I try to live each day with care,

But I know my time won't last so long there.

My days are short and my weeks go by,

I know my life will soon be cut down high.

My time won't last forever, I know,

And soon I'll be cut down low.

My life is short, my days are brief,

But I know that I'll find peace in belief. - Anonymous

Wind

James 4:14 asks, "What is your life?" Job 7:7 answers, "O remember that my life is wind:

mine eye shall no more see good."

I like to see the effects of the wind blowing through trees and tall grass or hay fields. I like to feel it blow on my face. I can remember when I was young that I would have the window down in the back seat of my parents' car with my arm hanging out allowing the wind to move it about. I would push against it and then relax allowing it to move my arm. I could see the affects of the wind even if I could not see the wind. This certainly helped me with understanding the Holy Spirit, Someone I could not see, but could certainly see the affects.

Wind moves quickly and then is gone. It is here and then gone. This is like life. It goes by so quickly. The weatherman will say that we will have sustained winds at a certain mile per hour. How long can a tree, house, etc., stand against the strain of the wind? What sustains you?

We refer to someone who is all talk as a windbag. Am I a lot of hot air? Do I do a lot of talking but not much action?

Wind blows in a specific direction. Our life is headed in a specific direction. Where are we blowing? Where is our life headed? What about my family? How are those relationships going? What direction is my marriage headed? What about my relationships with my children or other family members?

The wind comes and is gone. You can feel the affects of it even if you cannot see it. But just like that it moves on. So goes life.

Hurricanes come and sometimes do incredible damage but eventually they leave. The damage is still there, but the wind which caused it has moved on. Tornadoes are the same. At the moment of impact, they are horrifying. But soon they move on and the sun will reappear. There are times in our lives that we sustain heavy damage from events and circumstances. How are we able to continue on? How are we able to deal with what has happened? How we face difficulties reveals a lot about our character.

Everyone enjoys a gentle breeze especially when it is warm. Sometimes we need to get out of the house or office and get a breath of fresh air. It is refreshing. It clears the lungs. Sometimes we refer to someone as a breath of fresh air. They are new and exciting and have new or fresh ideas.

Wind often has an impact. It can be very strong or subtle changes depending on the strength of the wind. What impact are you having in your home? Are you impacting your spouse, children, grandchildren? What impact are you having in your community, church, and school? What differences are you making?

Some winds are very strong and can blow things a way. It can pick you up and blow you and even your neighborhood away. We can be blown away spiritually, mentally, and emotionally as well. If we are rooted and grounded in the Word and in our faith, that helps us to be able to withstand even the strongest of storms that come into our lives.

Some people say that they will never change. That is so sad because they stop growing. They also lose the opportunity to be like Christ. We need to always be changing ever growing. We are to continue to have the

mind of Christ become our mind. That is an ongoing
process that takes time.

My life is like wind that passes

Through valleys, over hills

It swirls and swoops an sways

In an ever-changing thrill

It brings some days of sorrow

And says of joy and glee

Sometimes I can't quite catch it

And I feel so lost at sea

But I keep on going, ever onward

To see what lies ahead

I can't control the wind

But I can steer my stead

Sometimes I get caught in a gust

My path becomes unclear

But I just close my eyes and feel

And hope for a new year

My life is like wind that passes

Sometimes it's strong and fast

But I'll take it journey by journey

Til the very end at last. - Anonymous

Nothing

James 4:14 asks, "What is your life?" Psalms 39:5 answers, "Indeed, You have made my days as handbreadths, and my age is as nothing before You; certainly every man at his best state is but vapor."

One thing that my dad told me over and over was to never let your car get below a quarter of a tank of gas. He would always keep his truck and cars between half and full. Of course, I would run it down as low as possible. One day, I ran out. This was before cell phones. So, I am walking down the road heading towards the nearest gas station. And guess who drives by, yep, my dad. He pulls over, and for a moment I thought about just keep walking. So, I got into the car. And, he did not say a word. He didn't have to. Lesson learned. I pass on the same advice to my own children today. When you are out of gas, you are out of gas. You are empty. There is nothing left to keep the vehicle moving. When you run out of gas, the car will stop. The same is true with you.

Eighty years of life compared to eternity is nothing comparatively speaking. It is soon

gone, where eternity, is outside of time.

My life is as nothing, a fleeting thought

A transient moment in time, hard to be caught

A flicker of light that fades with each breath

A spark that's extinguished with every death

My life is as nothing, a life of pain

A struggle of darkness that's never the same

A life of sorrow that's here and then gone

A life of hurt that can never be won

My life is as nothing, a broken dream

A life of hope that's never been seen

A life of failure that can't be undone

A life of despair that can never be won

My life is as nothing, a fading hope

A life that's been forgotten, a life that won't cope

A life of emptiness, a life of despair

A life that's been lost and no one to care - Anonymous

An Eagle that hasteth to her prey

James 4:14 asks, "What is your life?" Job 9:26

answers, "They pass by like swift ships,

like an eagle swooping on its prey."

An eagle is a majestic and powerful creature. I can

see why it was chosen as America's mascot animal. It

swoops down quickly to get its prey. It is said that the eagle

can see its prey as far as three miles away. It spots it from

way in the sky and can see the slightest movement. The

eagle makes its move and snatches it with her feet, takes it back to the nest, and then finishes it. She uses it to feed her family.

The prey usually never sees the eagle coming until it is too late. Sometimes life sneaks up on us. We never see it coming until the end. And then, it is too late.

My life is like an eagle that goes after its prey

It soars high above the sky and never delays

It chases after its goal with a powerful grace

And never stops until it's achieved its fate.

It swoops and dives with focused intent

It knows the prize it will soon be sent

A life of success and all it can bring

Is what the eagle will always seek.

My life is like an eagle that flies without fail

It never stops, no matter the gale

The winds of change can never deter

It follows its plan, no matter the weather.

My like is like an eagle, a graceful sight to see

It soars ever higher and never stops till the end

I take the time to appreciate this journey

And find the courage to go after my dreams. - Anonymous

A Swift Runner

James 4:14 asks, "What is your life?" Job 9:25 answers, "Now my days are swifter than a

runner; they flee away, they see no good."

I love track and field as a sport. In fact, I would say

that it is probably my favorite sport. The main reason is that

track and field offer a lot of variety and the majority of

people can find something that they might enjoy doing. If

you can run fast, then there are the sprints. Perhaps you can run for a long time, distances. Of course, there are the marathons for those who love to run forever. You can also jump such as the hurdles, long jump, high jump, long jump, and pole vault. If none of those things interest you, then you might enjoy throwing things: javelin, discus, shot and hammer.

It is exciting to watch the athletes compete and, especially to watch the race unfold. Will the leader be able to hold on to the lead? Is someone in the back going to make a move and pull in front? Your heart might race, and you can yell and holler for your favorite runner. But the race is soon finished. The runners cross the finish line. The times will tell how they finished.

Job compares our life to how fast the runner runs. There is a lot of excitement built up for the start of the race. The runner runs as fast and as long as they can. Then it is done. The same is true with life. It moves along swiftly until it is over. The important question to ask, is how did we run? Did we run our best? Were we able to complete the race? Did we falter or give up?

There is a lot of mental preparation that takes place before a race begins. The athlete thinks about how they are going to run, what their strategy might be. We must think about this race of life, and how we are going to run it. There must be consideration given to why we run and Who gives us the strength and stamina to run.

My life is like a swift runner

Picking up speed and gaining momentum

The pace is steady, but never dull

Every turn and bend is a new thrill

I dash and soar, leaping over obstacles

My feet pound the pavement with purpose

The path is winding, but I never tire

My energy and enthusiasm are ever-renewed

I am a swift runner, with a mission to achieve

My destination is unknown,

But I am determined to reach it

My life is a marathon,

And I am running with all my heart

I am a swift runner,

Always looking forward,

Never looking back. - Anonymous

Made in the USA
Columbia, SC
17 July 2023

20135691R10065